Coping With

Bereavement

Letters To My Wife In Heaven

Philip Hill

chipmunkapublishing
the mental health publisher

Published by
Chipmunkapublishing
PO Box 6872
Brentwood
Essex CM13 1ZT
United Kingdom

http://www.chipmunkapublishing.com

Edited by Tom Parmiter

ISBN   978-1-84991-826-8

Chipmunkapublishing gratefully acknowledge the support of Arts Council England.

ABOUT THE AUTHOR

Philip Hill was the youngest of a family of four and was born on the same day as his twin brother Paul. His elder brother was Peter and sister Anita, Philip never saw his father but was reunited with his mother on a visit to her care home when he was 14 years old. Philip and Paul were brought up by foster parents Albert and Jessica alongside their aoptive sister Lynn.

Separated from his natural mother at critical early stage and neglected in a children's home Philip was behind in achieving key academic and emotional developmental milestones.

Crucial to his later development was his twenty year marriage to Geraldine who had mental health issues which is something she had in common with her husband. They both supported one another and found it both difficult to live together and difficult to live apart.

When Geraldine died suddenly of liver cancer in the summer of 2011 naturally Philip was distraught and sought to write down his feelings as part of the bereavement process. While he continues to grieve Philip is anxious to share part of his coping strategies with the reader whilst informing the world at large what a beautiful person his wife was,

Philip has struggled with mental illness all his life and has documented his journey from unemployed outpatient via higher education and social care work experience to his current professional social worker role. This is detailed in his autobiography ' Living Out of The Book'(2008) and his novel 'Dopamine Clouds over Knighton Park,'(2009).

PART ONE – PRELUDE TO LETTERS

A chronology of selected diary entries that detail events that led to the death of Geraldine.

I had kept a journal of reflections on my social work practice but from April 2011 I started to keep a daily note of the unfolding events as Geraldine's health deteriorated. The motive for keeping this so called diary was a coping strategy to deal with difficult feelings that were to accompany my wife's sudden deterioration in health at the beginning of May 2011. My writing was very intense and a very personal way of coping with some difficult events. Without a bereavement support worker always on hand it was the only way I could cope. This developed into writing letters to Geraldine once she passed away on the 24th August 2011. Here are the most informative extracts from that diary.

15th May 2011

I arrived home for a second week in a row to find out that Geraldine had been in bed all day. It had only been three weeks ago since I went with her to Porthcrawl. But now she said she lay there most of the day and she had not ventured out of the flat. Every time she walked to the kitchen she felt dizzy and had to restrict her time there. I advised her to go to the doctor but she said she would be okay. I now had to shop for her every day.

16th July 2011

Five days before I had begun to notice that Geraldine was losing weight and turning a yellow complexion. She had previously arranged to see a doctor today but I wanted it brought forward a couple of days. When I told I had organised an appointment 4 days earlier she had a massive rant.

The night before that appointment I sat her on the sofa and told her I had some bad news. When I divulged my observations she double checked in the mirror and started to cry.

When we finally went to the GP I noticed that Geraldine was in the consulting room for almost an hour. When she came out, she told me 'You've got your own way I've been sent to hospital. Quick let's go home and pack and then take a taxi there.'

She barked out her orders of what to pack (including four toothbrushes and no toothpaste). I then ordered the taxi.

While we were waiting I offered to pray for her. As I did so I broke down in tears. Geraldine then had the strength from somewhere to pray for me as I sobbed uncontrollably.

As we were waiting to be seen by a doctor Geraldine said, 'I know it won't come to this but if I do die, I will leave everything to you. Let my friends have a choice of what they want from my belongings though.'

I stayed with her till 11 pm by which time she had still not been seen by a doctor.

17th July 2011

I got a call from Geraldine at 8am in the morning to say that she had been finally seen at 1pm and had woken her up. 'Don't forget to bring me a 'Woman Alive,' (*Christian magazine for women*).

18th July 2011

Brought Geraldine a get well card, grapes, a Sunday Observer and a load of other goodies. She seemed in good spirits but told me off for not brushing my teeth.

19th July 2011

Geraldine phoned me at 8am in the morning again. She told me the news I had been dreading; they had found lots of spots on the liver.

I do not know yet whether it is terminal. They have told her they need to carry out more scans.

Phoned my boss to tell him the news; told him I would not be at work for a few days.

20th July 2011

Watched 'Clash of the Titans' together (the old version).

We had a good chuckle at the naff special effects.

22nd July 2011

Geraldine's friend Deborah visited and smuggled in a Guinea Pig in her handbag which caused us all to have a quiet fit of laughter.

23rd July 2011.

I turned up after work to be told by Geraldine that she was being discharged with no further treatment and with the results of the scans pending.

I had a problem getting Geraldine to climb the stairs when we got back because she was so weak.

5th August 2011

I went with Geraldine to the hospital outpatient's appointment. She became distressed and dizzy during the wait for the appointment and they rushed her in to the outpatient's appointment early. The specialist consultant was there and by the expression on his face you knew he had the shittest job in the world to tell people about their liver cancer prognosis.

He told Geraldine straight, 'you'll be doing quite well if you are still alive at Christmas.' Geraldine replied, 'At least I know now. I have made it up with God, I just worry about those left behind,' at which point I cried on cue. The nurse was there and she explained to Geraldine that for the purposes of applying for DLA Benefits they would put down that she had less than six months to live.

Geraldine then told me on waiting for the outpatients' ambulance to take her home that her wish was for Amy Winehouse to sing to her in heaven.

13th August 2011

I was watching Amy Winehouse on a Jools Holland special when I heard a cry. It was Geraldine unable to get off the toilet. It took ten minutes to mobilise her to her bed after which we were both in floods of tears.

14th August 2011

Geraldine was due to go to Deborah's for five days to give me in Geraldine's words 'some respite.'

She was leaving our flat when she fell down the stairs. She could not get up despite assistance from me and Deborah. She had the indignity of lying down in the hallway for nearly a full hour before the ambulance came.

When I returned home from the hospital I knew Geraldine would never come home again. She did not have the ability to climb those stairs again.

17th August 2011

Geraldine somehow seems distant when I visited her. Then the explanation – she had started to take morphine.

I tried to get her to sign forms for her benefits and was shocked she had lost the capacity to sign her own name.

18th August 2011

When I visited I was told by nursing staff that Geraldine had become a bit disorientated with time and place. She had had an unsettled night and was calling out in a demanding way, 'where's my husband'…

I was allowed to stay overnight that night in a make shift bed in hospital in Geraldine's en suite room.

Geraldine complained about my snoring but was glad to have me there.

19th August 2011

I was called by Geraldine's consultant on my mobile and told she had been moved to St Mary's Hospice. I challenged the consultant about why they weren't treating her in hospital but then he said the hospice was the best place for her. I broke down in tears in the workplace and was comforted by Juliet. I was advised by colleagues to go to the hospice and sign off sick.

I arrive at the hospice to find that the doctor and nurses are around the bed. Geraldine is in good spirits and I cry by her bedside. She describes to the doctor and nurses why she had to give up her job twenty three years ago.

I go away from the bed to speak to the doctor. The news is not good. Geraldine doesn't have much time left. I mull this over in the hospice café then on the way to returning to Geraldine's bed I find her sitting in a chair. She tells me off, constantly in frustration at being unable to get her up. However she can't get up from the chair and it takes an hour for a physiotherapist to be called and she uses a Zimmer frame to get Geraldine up, and once up Geraldine uses the frame competently to get back to bed.

I stay at the hospice for seven hours that day getting to know staff well. But the trip to the hospice garden that Geraldine wanted, it turns out she will never be well enough to do.

20th August 2011

The day starts well with a letter addressed to Geraldine explaining that she had the top levels of disability benefit. When I arrive at the hospital I find she does not have capacity to take this in.

I am told by nurses she has had an unsettled night.

Amanda, Wilf and Helen visit.

Helen promises Geraldine she will look after me then breaks down in floods of tears.

Amanda prays with Geraldine and brings flowers.

Geraldine cries out in pain and calls me to her bedside. 'Help me will you,' she says, 'you can help others but you can't help me.'

'Help me will you, help me, fly round the bed or something.'

'Don't look at me gormless, help me!'

I leave Geraldine's bedside in floods of tears.

Deborah then visits and comes away in tears. We hug and cry together.

Geraldine subsequently calls out in pain for help from Mummy, and Daddy (both of whom were dead).

She finally called out 'Holly help me.' She was even calling out to the cat.

I speak with the doctor. Geraldine has a matter of days to live and the nurses (with the doctor) plan to give her morphine intravenously.

I ask for a priest to be called urgently because this may be the last opportunity for her to realise she is being prayed for.

We pray then he consults me alone in the peace room and said he was sorry to see us in such circumstances.

21st August 2011

A letter arrived this morning from one of the main four banks telling me I was owed twelve thousand pounds compensation for the miss selling of Personal Loan Insurance. My initial feeling was one of elation and then I became despondent. Geraldine had lost mental capacity 48 hours previously. There was no way I could share the money with her. We had scrimped and saved throughout the whole of our marriage and now she would not even have the knowledge that I would be okay. I had tried to bring forward our last holiday together from Christmas to September but she would even be too ill to go on that excursion.

Geraldine's pen friend of 30 years Mary arrives and has not ever met Geraldine face to face and is confronted by someone who is almost comatose. I hug her and we both cry.

Ian and Annette, Anne and Heather all visit to be recognised briefly before Geraldine slips into sleep.

I visited Geraldine that day.

I held her hand and the tears fell down my cheeks. I struggled to say the words and as I did I cried, 'I love you.'

She said in a very serene way, 'Thank you,' and then fell into semi- consciousness. That was the last time I felt that I effectively communicated to Geraldine...

I can't sleep at home and end up going to the hospice to be with Geraldine overnight.

22nd August 2011

Emma the priest from our church visits Geraldine.

Geraldine hears our voices and briefly bolts upright. 'Oh Emma, nice to see you.' Then she falls back to sleep and we both pray for her.

23rd August 2011

11am

Geraldine called out from the side of the bed 'Can you do me a favour.' I knew she was in pain. I called the nurse on the onside bed monitor.
A nurse came and said they were working with another patient but would be there soon. Geraldine fidgeted in bed as she writhed in

discomfort. I felt helpless and told her time after time to wait for the nurse. It was about twenty minutes to wait and it seemed like forever as I watched my wife struggle in pain.

After diagnosing the issues two nurses went away and came back another twenty minutes later with a syringe which they injected into her leg. Geraldine was then fumbling at the side of the bed. I was clueless what to do. One of the nurses then said she's trying to touch you. I reached out to her hand and we held hands for ten minutes. That was the last I saw of Geraldine.

Geraldine is visited by Wilf and Helen and grunts acknowledgement of the prayer that Helen recites.

PART TWO

LETTERS TO GERALDINE

24th August 2011

Dear Geraldine,

I write this knowing you have just passed away. I was on the way into the city centre on the bus when I got a call from St Mary's Hospice. 'I am afraid to say that Geraldine passed away this morning.'

I broke down and cried on the phone. My voice cracked as I struggled to make conversation with the nurse at the other end. I told her I would ring back to arrange a viewing of your body.

I phoned my adoptive sister Lynn who urged me to cancel the cancer screening that afternoon. After talking to her and finding her so empathic and understanding I phoned back St Mary's Hospice to say that I would be there in little under 4 hours to view your body with my foster mother and Lynn.

I arrived to be told I could not view your body unless I took financial responsibility for the funeral arrangements. My sister knowing my precarious financial position tried to explore the possibility of the welfare system taking over financial control. I then remember having a rant saying there were no circumstances I would allow you to have a cheapo funeral. I wanted the funeral to be just as we had planned.

I remember going into the room with my foster mother where your body lay. I have never really seen eye to eye on every issue with my foster mother. But she came 500 miles from Scotland to support me at this difficult time and now we were closer that we had ever been. We hugged each other crying as we did so. Then I kissed your lips twice but they felt like solid blocks of ice because your soul had long departed to another dimension.

I arrived at St Martins Tea Lounge and told Tom Thompson you have died and within half an hour I received phone calls from both the Rector Stewart and the Assistant Curate Emma. They tell me they are to support me and I arrange with Emma a time to meet her to plan the order of service.

I wish I could still kiss you now. Wherever you are I love you with all my heart.

Love

Philip

26th August 2011

Dear Geraldine,

I go to the doctors and meet Dr Shah. He sits with me for quarter of an hour as I describe in a deadpan way that I feel completely cried out of tears. I ask him for time off work and he gives me a month off and gives me an NHS guide to bereavement.

I then go to Halliday Street (just off Broad Street), meet my foster mother and brother at the registry office and after a short wait we go into a private room where we discuss the death certificate. Eventually I sign your death certificate without any tears because as I explained in my last letter I am all cried out and cannot summon any tears.

We go to the undertakers with my father who arrives late at the registry office.

We then go to the undertakers in Yardley.

The funeral is arranged for September the 6th on my insistence that some of your friends need to return from holiday before any service is held.

I insist on St Martin's as the venue for the funeral in line with your wishes and I am told in no uncertain terms that you are a very privileged person to have the funeral service there.

I decide on an order of service and bring in my favourite photo of you and manage to agree everything we had talked about when we planned what you wanted.

29th August 2011

August Bank Holiday

Dear Geraldine,

I went to Greenbelt 2011 (the Christian arts festival at Cheltenham Race course).

The greatest gift you gave me was my Christian faith. You wanted so much to go to this festival once more but did not maintain your health long enough to come with me.

We stayed there to camp for the three days of the festival many times. The last time was in 2004 when Billy Bragg was headlining. The one year there was a storm and overnight rain. And do you remember that apart from trying to get some sleep with me snoring our tent was one of the few not to collapse?

It is strange going round familiar haunts such at the 'Tiny Tea Tent', The Jesus Arms, the craft stalls and not having you there with me. I am not emotional though, I feel I have cried myself out over the last seven days of your life and have no more emotion to give. I am with my brother who is supporting and as you know he is not a Christian so I can't do a lot of the joint prayer sessions that we used to have together.

I enter a meditation space in the main grandstand and see a counsellor who prays for me.

I feel an emptiness inside because you are not with me.

I pray for your soul dear Geraldine.

Love

Philip

5th September 2011

Dear Geraldine,

I remember our conversation on the 14th of August 2011.

You had just spent an hour being unable to mobilise after falling down the stairs of our 1st floor flat. You had agreed with Deborah that you had taken it out on those closest to you, namely me.

By the time you arrived at the hospital I realised you would never return home which caused me to cry yet again.

We had a brief conversation about how you wanted the funeral arrangements to be. We agreed that Vaughan Williams should be the music used to the procession of the coffin. I hummed the tune of 'Dives and Lazarus' and you agreed that would be good. You also wanted

'Love Divine All Loves Excelling' as one of the hymns because we mistakenly thought that was by Vaughan Williams. Then you said you wanted something by Graham Kendrick and we agreed on 'Shine Jesus Shine'.

You said you wanted the funeral service to take place at St Martin's to which I was pleasantly surprised.

Finally your wish was for the poem 'Stop the Clocks' by W.H. Auden.

When we arrived at the undertakers two days after your earthly existence he was taken aback by my request to have the service at St Martin's Church. When I told him that I had been a parishioner there for 13 years he told me in no uncertain terms that Geraldine was a very privileged woman.

You had remained strangely silent on whether you wanted to be cremated or buried. I decided on a cremation because I could honestly see myself visiting the graveside for years to come without moving on. I was in HMV music store when I felt you were trying to suggest to me subliminally that an Aretha Franklin track '(You Make Me Feel Like) A Natural Woman,' would be a good departing track from the funeral service. I played this single endlessly for the next week because it made me feel better about my role in your life.

I wrote a Eulogy over a week or so before your funeral. Emma the priest thought it was okay and asked me if I would feel able to read it out at the service. I hope you approve.

Love

Philip

6th September 2011 - The Funeral

Eulogy for Geraldine Hill – A Tribute From Her Husband

INTRODUCTION

When I married Geraldine I was an immature 25 year old who had only explored the depths of his emotions twice and that had caused me to have two nervous breakdowns. I encountered the public face of Geraldine when I first met her. She was effortless and confident. She had just recently moved into specialist accommodation for people with mental health issues. She had confined herself to her room but staff had bargained with her to come down that evening to watch Dallas. So we met because of Dallas.

Initially because of her immaculate appearance and her apparent confidence I mistakenly thought she was a healthcare professional. After about fifteen minutes we were left alone together. I tried to be as calm and pleasant as I could be and when I did send her a Valentine's card a week later she told me she had unresolved feelings for someone else.

Because Geraldine had been straightforward with me I found it easy to deal with this setback. However about a fortnight later we went to Aston Hall together. We came out to a bench and then I knew it was serious because she kissed me for the first time. That was the start of our 21 year relationship.

Once I got to know Geraldine however I found that the effortless confidence she seemed to exude was a front beneath which she agonised over every social interaction that she prepared for.

I was quick off the mark and asked her to marry me within six months of our relationship. She warned me at this stage that I would not just be marrying her but all her accompanying hang ups which I was to find out were panic attacks caused by anxiety, eating problems caused by bulimia and mood swings caused by depression. Throughout our marriage Geraldine taught me to be more patient, as well as to be a gentler, kinder and more caring person.

Our marriage had its ups and down and we never seemed to be able to live together or apart. Watching her die I wished I could become a surrogate cancer sufferer so that I could take some of her pain. I have never watched someone suffer like I did Geraldine during the last week of her life.

It always seemed that me and Geraldine needed a good argument and the real prospect of splitting up to appreciate how much we truly loved one another.

Reading eulogy below at the funeral was the best tribute I was able to give but sometimes my feelings are so overwhelmed it is beyond words

EULOGY

Geraldine was born in Hereford on the 3rd December 1958 to a mother who named her Patricia Ellick. Her natural parents felt they could not look after her and she was adopted in Birmingham. She then became called Geraldine Blizard and was cared for by adoptive parents John and Stella and her adoptive sister Georgina (whose children Richard and Charlotte she later became aunt to). Gary Bland became her brother in law once Georgina married.

Geraldine was bought up in Kings Heath. She was bright at school and left with a couple of O levels and went straight to work on leaving school.

After watching a feature film about University Challenge called 'Starter for Ten' she felt she had missed out on the student life and that was one of her few regrets. She could have gone to Moseley College of Art at 14 but lacked the confidence to follow it through. She worked in an office before progressing to a support worker at what was then called the Employment Preparation Unit for people with Learning Disabilities. Eventually however in 1988 the emergence of her mental health issues meant she had to retire. In 1992 she tried working briefly for Leisure Forum and eventually retired again prematurely.

Geraldine wanted to be remembered as a successful person. She then seemed to pause after stating this to reflect on the mental health issues that she had had, her eating disorder, depression, and anxiety. In terms of qualifications, high powered jobs and being at peace with herself then perhaps she did not achieve these conventional measures of success. She felt on reflection that by having to confront her challenging mental health issues which affected her on a daily basis that she had demonstrated relentless bravery. How she had the courage to walk into Sainsbury's in Kings Heath, when she had had countless panic attacks there previously, I will never know. She used public transport with great difficulty because of the regular panic attacks. She had what some call social phobia, a genuine fear of social situations, which caused anxiety and was constantly asking me if she had interacted with other people okay. She was quaking inside when in fact she had seemed from an outsiders view so effortless in her conversation. From meeting her for the first time twenty years ago I had initially thought she was a weak and fragile person but over time I appreciated the reserves of fortitude and determination she needed to get out and about in the community.

However as her husband I have to say that she was the silent partner and backbone of my 3 postgraduate degrees and my career as a professional support worker and then professional social worker providing both practical support and a listening ear. She typed three to four hundred pages of transcript for interviews I undertook as a research student as well as my research diary. It is a travesty my research degree has not got her name on it.

.

She was also an enduring and constant support to a dozen or so friends whom she sustained with her chatty, warm and supportive e mails, long phone calls, and letters. To people at Friendship Housing and Bright Sparks she seemed effortless in her ability to socialise but to her close friends and to her husband they knew the secret turmoil of those seemingly effortless interactions. Those that knew her well knew she was intelligent, articulate, warm and friendly, a troubled but gentle soul. Geraldine had the most beautiful spoken voice.

The biggest thing me and Geraldine had in common was our Christian faith.

In the end Geraldine was not devastated by the cancer diagnosis. As she said to me 'I have made my peace with God, I just worry about those I leave behind and how they will cope.' She identified with the poem 'Footprints' because she felt carried through her ordeal with cancer by God even though she experienced great pain and disorientation towards the end.

And so Geraldine amongst those gathered today your life was a success. You were a successful wife and a successful friend and the world was a better place with you in it.

6th September 2011

Dear Geraldine,

You know what an exhibitionist I am. Reading your eulogy out amongst the mourners would be a claim to an Andy Warhol like 15 minutes of fame. But when it came to it I almost bottled it. In the preceding hymn I kept breaking down in floods of tears. So when it came to it I kept calm and read the Eulogy out like I had practiced it ten times before.

Emma the presiding priest was efficient as ever and made a good impression on those present. She told me to tell you she understands your problems with the Church of England and she has problems too, even though she works for them. Deborah had problems with your choice of poem 'Stop the Clocks' By W.H. Auden though she said she'd take that up with you in the afterlife.

Anne did a brief eulogy that described your fun loving nature.

I had about twenty sympathy cards given to me on the day. As per your wishes nearly everyone turned up in a colour other than black. I had a white Marks and Spencer blazer with a psychedelic shirt and white trousers. My brother Paul, you know what a copycat he is, had an identical psychedelic but on my instruction wore a different colour blazer.

You had a good turn out, so good in fact that we almost ran out of orders of service and I ordered seventy copies.

You know when I told you St Peter would not let you in at the Pearly Gates unless you started forgiving people. Well, I invited your sister to the funeral and like many people in your life she is someone you fell out with. A funeral should be a place where people we have known can make their peace. Sorry if I messed things up. You had by all accounts a very moving service. There were some people you only became acquainted with briefly but you made such an impression on them that they felt they had to pay their final respects. My father apologised to me and indirectly to you that he had never taken the time and trouble to understand your disability. My mother said she cried more at your funeral than her own mothers a month before.

Stewart took the service at the crematorium and I decided to use the classical piece from the British Airways advert that I know was your favourite opera as the entrance music.

I did the best that I could to give you a good send off.

Love

Philip

17th September 2011

Dear Geraldine,

I have been in Scotland for ten days and it is as though I have forgotten about you. Nothing in my parents' cottage reminds me of you. If I had not seen your dead body I would swear I was coming home to you.

It has taken me 7 years to pay off a twenty four grand loan that financed my student years and we have both had to tighten our belts. It is a cruel blow that I cannot share my new found financial stability with you. I can finally afford to give you the holiday of a lifetime and you are not here. Surely god cannot be in charge of this type of cruel fate.

Your sister told me that only the good die young which doesn't say much for the rest of us left behind.

I am trying to set up a legacy at Leicester University in your name. A prize for students who overcome difficult odds or something is what I am proposing. I never want to forget and can't wait to get home to be around things that remind me of you.

Love

Philip

20th September 2011

Dear Geraldine,

You know when we compromised on bread while out shopping?

I liked white bread and you like wholemeal. So we compromised on granary loaves. You particularly liked the 'Burgen' loaf from Sainsbury's.

I came into Sainsbury's local in Moseley (our usual haunt) and what should strike my attention was that two loaves of Burgen fell off the shelf as I walked by. Are you interceding for me or something? I am sure it was you that pushed those loaves off the shelf in front of me. It's your way of saying look after yourself.

Please show yourself again.

Love

Philip

21st September 2011

Dear Geraldine,

I know you often got quite angry with me, particularly towards the end.

I am sorry I did not take the level of pride in my appearance that you did. I wished I had taken that extra attention to detail to show that I cared about us rather than my own self absorbed feelings.

I am sorry that I did not acknowledge your bravery more than once. I pushed you too hard at times particularly in the early years of our relationship. When I got round to reading your journal, which I found just after you had died, I realised how much fortitude was necessary just for you to manage your food intake (you were a member of overeaters anonymous) and how much courage you had to pluck up to travel on buses after experiencing countless panic attacks on public transport before.

If it is any consolation I would not have lasted in social work without you. You taught me patience, understanding and empathy for others.

May you be in a dimension where you no longer face those daily struggles.

Love

Philip

23rd September 2011

Dear Geraldine,

I am constantly worried that these letters do not get to you and that our physical dimension is the only one there is with no heaven or a hell. I keep asking everyone I know does your soul still exist and if so in what dimension.

My prayers were answered tonight by a science programme that explained string theory. As you know Einstein's laws about the speed of light and the behaviour of the universe explain phenomena adequately above atomic level. But at sub atomic level quantum mechanics which is the theory of best fit is at odds with Einstein's theory of Relativity. In his lifetime Einstein tried to reconcile his theories of relativity with quantum mechanics but failed to find a theory for everything. The closest the scientific community has to a theory for everything is string theory.

As you know, the physical dimensions of our universe are in 4 dimensions, 3D plus time the fourth dimension.

The idea, as you know, behind string theory is that this universe is only one string of a violin and that the other strings represent separate dimensions. There could be according to scientists up to 11 dimensions. If this is not a theory of god then strike me down now.

As well as this there has been a recent headline in the Guardian about scientists in mainland Europe discovering that there is a possibility that sub atomic particles known as neutrino's may travel faster than the speed of light which undermines Einstein's theories. If this proves to be true that relationship between cause and effect is broken and that this may point to the existence of another dimension.

I don't know which dimension you are in but please continue to watch over me.

Love

Philip

P.S — Reading in December's Guardian the search for the possibility of a 'god particle' may have reached a crucial stage. As you know this is the particle that collides with sub atomic particles to give them actual mass.

25th September 2011

Dear Geraldine,

I have been trying to get you to intercede in my life again without success. I have tried everything to get your attention like leaving my pants in the toilet (that used to make you so cross) and leaving my flat without tidying up. But still you do not intercede.

Yours in desperation

Philip

9th October 2011

Dear Geraldine,

I have invited your friends Deborah and Anne to come round to sort your stuff.

I tried to throw away all your clothes but I couldn't. I kept the yellow dressing gown because you always looked so snug in it.

I could not throw any of your night dresses away because your looked so sexy in them.

I cried when I tried to throw your green overcoat away. The countless times you had told me off in that coat. Anne took the blue overcoat.

Anne had the first pick of your books while Deborah had the first choice of the candles. I did not realise you kept every single Christmas card from me and all my love letters.

We admired your school reports which had the usual throw away phrase of 'could do better.'

I dropped your remaining books and clothes at the two Oxfam shops in Moseley.

I hope this is okay with you.

Love

Philip

16th October 2011 – the Internment of Geraldine's Ashes at St Martin's Church

Dear Geraldine,

I have made a bit of a gamble on your last wishes. I thought that if you wanted your funeral at St Martin's church you would also want your ashes interred there as well.

There was a decent turnout of about thirty people. The Rector Stewart said it would be a short service but it would not be rushed. The same reading that was used at the funeral service was also used here. It's that reading where St Paul in a roundabout way eventually says 'nothing can separate us from the love of god.' It was read out by Emma.

Deborah then read a poem which I thought was a bit intense for the funeral but ideal for the interment of your ashes. The poem was about your constant struggle with death in your life and now you were finally released from that struggle.

As the ashes were poured the light streamed through the window in the chapel as your remains were placed in the foundations of the church.

A lot of people thanked Deborah for her poem afterwards and I left with a tear in my eye.

I always feel your presence when I go to church. I light a candle in the chapel for you every Sunday.

God Bless

Philip

7th November 2011

Dear Geraldine,

I got told today I am not coping at work. It is true though that I have been spontaneously having crying fits at work. David said I am okay on some days but not all the time. I had a panic attack when I had to do a transition meeting at a school at short notice.

Please intercede for me.

Love

Philip

13th November 2011

Dear Geraldine,

I went to church today to the Remembrance service and arrived early so that I could keep the two minutes silence.

Thought and prayed for you as well.

Love

Philip

15th November 2011

Dear Geraldine,

I had a tricky time in therapy today finally opening up about my affairs of the heart some of which I had not told you about. It got so intense the therapist ran out of tissues. I will tell you more in my next letter.

Love

Philip

25th November 2011

Dear Geraldine,

Work is overtaking my life. I leave the house as you know (you used to get me up at 7am) at 7.30am and don't return till 6pm. I am sorry that over the last few years that I seemed preoccupied with my job. Many times I would come home and go to sleep and wake up just as you were going to bed.

I wish I had concentrated a little less on my own personal development when we were married and used the debt I accumulated during my student years on a holiday of a lifetime to the holy land. You always wanted to go there.

Using the definition of adultery that Jesus himself used, I was guilty of many affairs of the heart during my marriage, not all of whom you were aware about. It is true that I remained faithful to you apart from our three month separation in 1996 when I mislead you that I was starting another relationship which of course I wasn't.

In many ways I took you for granted and when you were ill only then did I realise what I was losing. You remember that I cried during our prayer together on the sofa before you were first admitted to hospital with cancer. I can honestly say that since then I have never cried more over anyone else in my life. It did not feel appropriate to cry in front of you but I could not help myself.

When they let you home before you went into the hospice I found it difficult being with you and without you those weeks. When I sat at your bedside not knowing what to say, I did not know what to say to someone who was dying. I tried to cook you food to the best of my ability, even though in the early stages of my marriage you said you would never eat anything I cooked for you.

Please forgive me Geraldine, I am such a fool. There have been times when I told too many people about your illness and I didn't respect your dignity. Please believe I never meant to cause you anguish. You always have carried yourself in a more dignified way than me. I often broke your confidences because I was not as discreet as you.

I lied to you when you were in the hospice and told you that I had not told Fifi about your diagnosis when I had. I felt bad about that. Fifi is one of my friends you detest the most and I lied to you because the truth would have caused you more anguish.

I love you. I try not to hurt you but sometimes I am like a clumsy bull in a china shop. Whatever dimension you are in please forgive me my foolish ways.

All my love

Philip

28th November 2011

Dear Geraldine,

It's approaching your birthday which as you know is this Saturday, the 3rd of December. I never forgot your birthday all the years we were married and I am not about to now.

I am meeting up with your close friend Anne and we are going to the chapel at St Martin's church to light a candle each for you. Anne said you deliberately chose St Martin's for your interment because of the proximity of the Christmas German Market so you could go out and continue your annual retail therapy.

We will go shopping there as well. I have phoned all your close friends and asked them to light a candle on December the 3rd.

As you know you wanted me to take up the flute again so I will buy a brand new silver flute and pretend it's a Christmas present from you and start lessons in the New Year.

Love

Philip

30th November 2011

Dear Geraldine,

I went on Strike today to stop the government robbing my pension pot. Most people are reconciled to the fact that we need to pay more for our pensions. But to pay more, work longer and get less is definitely over the top.

I was too depressed to get up and slept in till 12 midday. I should have really picketed my workplace but after last time when I was the only person in our team to do so I started asking myself, what's the point of winding up people who aren't even union members?

Thank you for the Christmas present you always wanted to get for me, namely a flute. The shop had no brand new flutes so I bought a second hand reconditioned American flute with a solid silver headpiece. You would have approved I know you would.

Whatever dimension you are in I hope you will be able to hear me playing to you.

Love

Philip

3rd December 2011

Dear Geraldine,

I had my haircut and beard trim today. I had to look my best for your special day, what would have been your 53rd birthday.

I met with Anne Woodford today and we both lit candles where your ashes as interred. I almost burnt my fingers in the process.

Anne talked about you incessantly and made me appreciate how much you really loved me. She said you were possessive and on occasion threatened to lay into a woman who was touching my face but relented when you found out she was only applying face paint. I know you disapproved of my friendship with Fifi but I did not have an affair with her.

She told me how you really fancied me from our earliest meeting. You confided a great deal in her. You told her how I came back early from our days out so we could watch 'Strictly' together. You always wrote your thank you letters on Christmas telling people I had gone to sleep and I was snoring.

Christmas was invented for you. You reveled in mulled wine, chestnuts and the German Christmas market. Myself and Anne went round the market thinking of you and your insatiable appetite for candles, soaps, and other nick-nacks.

I love you with all my heart. My appetite for life has diminished; I just want to die so I can be close to you.

All my love

Philip

4th December 2011

Dear Geraldine,

I went Christmas shopping today and my debit card became tatty by the end of the day after being plugged into countless chip and pin machines. This piece of plastic must have been hit harder than a flurry of punches from Mohammed Ali himself.

I bought the entire stock of religious cards at Clinton's and then decided to try if I could get all my Christmas presents at HMV. I must have added something like 10,000 points to my PURE HMV reward card that day. Then armed with a giant HMV and Clinton's bags I attended the Fire Service annual Christmas service and met my previous manager Sue. She told me that when she had found out you had died she had to go home from work she was so shocked.

I caught up with her latest strategy to move to

Dorset. She is awaiting the results of an interview to work on a Dementia ward down there.

The nativity scene was enacted by children of Mayfield Special School. You would have been touched by the way in which one of the soloists got carried away and sung their part three times in a moving out of tune unplanned repeat performance. The story, entitled 'The Kiss', was that despite the attentions of the shepherds and the three wise men the baby Jesus kept crying until his mother Mary gave him a kiss.

The choir sang and the Fire service band played a selection of poptastic carols accompanied by the usual readings.

Hope you're enjoying a mince pie on me whatever dimension you are in.

Love

Philip

6th December 2011

Dear Geraldine,

Went for the results of my biopsy today and was given the all clear. Going back to the hospital where you were treated was an eerie experience. Nothing has changed. I waited for nearly an hour and a half to be seen. When I had my height and weight taken I thought that the result might be in doubt. I was half wanting to be diagnosed with cancer so I could see you sooner rather than later.

The clinician asked me whether I drank or not. He said that drink often caused the bowel to be inflamed. I said that I had started to drink heavily since your death and then he asked me how long you had been dead. I did not expect that question so I could not stop myself from crying. I know that you would not want to see me distressed but I do get caught out sometimes though most of the time I seem okay.

I arrived home to find a lovely letter from the undertakers W.H Painter. They have put up a memorial Christmas tree. So I will pop by and put a remembrance card from you on it.

I love you still more than ever.

Philip

8th December 2011

Dear Geraldine,

Everything seems to irritate me at work. I wonder whether I can hold out to the Christmas break. I think constantly how empty Christmas will be without you. My brother has volunteered to be with me over the Christmas break but it won't be the same. Buying presents for you was a pleasure because you were so easy to buy for. I remember the Christmas I bought you the Russian doll representing 5 of the Russian premiers you were so ecstatic. This Christmas I was going to buy you a Kindle e book reader, which I knew you wanted because you kept dropping hints; it would have been your brand new toy.

Christmas was made for you from your many indulgences in mulled wine, chestnuts and pretzels to our constant meetings at the German market so you could buy presents for others.

Being a vegetarian you put up with my constant need to buy frankfurters from one of those German take away stalls.

Do you remember the CBSO Christmas Choral Concert from last year, and the narrator Ben Fogle who had just been to the South Pole to film for the BBC in Captain Scott's footsteps and arrived to say that our record snowy weather was just like being there back in the Antarctica? You enjoyed that concert and if I remember it was the last one we went to. You insisted on an end row seat in case you had a panic attack and had to leave suddenly.

Then there were those silly hats we both wore on Christmas Day. My ritual was to watch 'It's a Wonderful Life' on Christmas Eve, followed by carols at King's. You always watched the DVD Tim Burton's 'Nightmare Before Christmas' because I found out belatedly you loved horror films. We always went to midnight mass at St

Anne's and you made sure I had a pork pie and a sherry before we went to bed.

You used to have so many presents that when we took turns you opened two presents to my every one because you were so popular amongst your friends they insisted on buying you a little something.

We went out for a meal last Christmas Day and I was so full I went to sleep and you had to put up with my snoring for the rest of the day.

I cherish the memories of our last Christmas together. You have a good Christmas whichever dimension you are in.

And by the way have a mulled wine on me.

Love

Philip

10th December 2011

Dear Geraldine,

I watched the 'Strictly' semi-finals on BBC1 and found that one of the couples are dancing to '(You Make Me Feel Like) A Natural Woman' by Aretha Franklin. Are you trying to communicate with me (the theme was used for your funeral)?

12th December 2011

Dear Geraldine,

Do you remember our 'in jokes' about Cliff Richard? I bought you a Cliff Richard birthday card which gave us both lots of laughter with him singing 'Happy Birthday to you.'

You remember that Christmas when Cliff got to number 1 with 'Saviour's Day'? We both groaned. Then to both our delights it was replaced as the New Year number one by Iron Maiden's 'Bring Your Daughter ...to the Slaughter'. Goody two shoes Cliff did not get his own way that year at least.

Can't find your favourite Christmas album 'Classic Christmas' but don't worry, I am looking after myself.

Love

Philip

Dear Geraldine,

Me and Paul went to the annual Christmas concert by the CBSO. You'll be delighted to learn that the narrator was the winner of that celebrity conducting competition, Sue Perkins. She conducted one of your favourite pieces by Leroy Anderson, 'Sleigh Ride'.

The children's chorus was as delightful as when we went last year. The Youth Chorus was good and the CBSO Chorus is always a good bet for an immaculate performance.

20th December 2011

Dear Geraldine,

I got a phone call from Anne Woodford. I was shocked to hear that she tuned into the radio station three times over the weekend to find the music to the procession of your coffin being broadcast namely 'Dives and Lazarus'. Are you trying to intercede in her life or something? I hope you are watching over me.

Love

Philip

MY FINAL LETTER

21ST December 2011

Dear Geraldine,

Today is the winter solstice. Every day for the next six months after this will be lighter and brighter. In writing to you over the last 4 months I have explored the very depths of my heart and opened up to you in a way I could not have when you were alive. I have done this because I am certain that your soul lives on out there in another dimension. I knew that before you died you believed in angels and now I believe you are an angel. But now I feel the time is ripe for letting go. Please continue through the godhead to watch over me. However I do not need constant reassurance of your presence in my life. I need Jesus and because you led me to him I feel that in following him I am meeting your will for me. I still find it difficult to go on without you but I also believe that both you and

God have a plan for me that in the depths of winter I cannot see but which will be revealed to me in time.

I can still feel you telling me off and nagging me for the usual offences such as tooth brushing, and general grooming. That is good because I would hate to feel that in our 21 and a half years together you had not molded and shaped me in a lasting way.

Before I sign off I would like to say I will always be inspired by your courage and your will to succeed. I know your faith was an important part of that inner resolve that you had.

Be assured I will always love you to the very depths of my being. Being very robotic when I first met you, you have taught me the very essence of what it is to be human.

I will always love you, may our souls meet again once more one day but until then,

Hugs and kisses from your loving husband,

Philip

P.S – I am asking my brother to wrap up some presents I bought for myself from you.

P.P.S – I will learn the flute and play music to you that only you can appreciate in eternity.

www.ingramcontent.com/pod-product-compliance
Lightning Source LLC
Chambersburg PA
CBHW030346030726
47499CB00003B/934